That was Then, This is Now

That was Then, This is Now

Just the Beginning

Branford L. Moton

Print information available on the last page.

Rev. date: 03/18/2016

To order additional copies of this book, contact:
Xlibris
1-888-795-4274
www.Xlibris.com
Orders@Xlibris.com
550610

Contents

Introduction

Before reading this book I just want to give
you a little piece of my life story.

I was born at St. Luke's Hospital on May 30, 1989. I was raised in
Cleveland, Ohio in the 105th and St. Clair area on Empire. As a young
child I kept journals for myself and wrote journals for school and these
things propelled me forward in taking an interest in writing poems.

I began to take writing more seriously at the age of seven-teen; while
in the 11th and 12th grade, attending Mayfield High School. This
is when I met Mrs. Lynn M. Connelly; she was my speech teacher,
and she influence me to pursue my creative writing skills.

Mrs. Connelly taught me various techniques on speaking and speech
pertaining to comprehending and analyzing what you read and
what you write. This gave me a great understanding of the art.
This is my first book and one of my greatest moments. I have put
countless hours and taken an immense amount of time to write it.

I am especially thankful for having great, motivated, spirit-filled people
pushing me forth to do what I love; and that's "floetic" words to share.

I have experienced many life events; some experiences
were good and some were bad; but with that I have written
good and invented great poems; I just dream about!

To my fellow book readers, book lovers, poetry readers and poetry
lovers, etc. And so forth; thanks for supporting me by purchasing this
book. It is my great legacy and life work that I invested in for six years.
I hope you all embrace everything I put into these poems; as well as
understanding where I come from. As a poet; i want you to know that
my words have meanings behind meanings; and that's my intent.

My Life
C.S.S.

In my life all I'm doing is living a struggle but as I grow
and get wise just like I have gotten baptized.

I want to build muscle I can't let this struggle get me down.

My self-esteem level is the one going down.

I don't want to carry against the world a frown.

But just like scientist say about gravity;

"What goes up must come down".

All I want to do is melt away or shut-down my problems
and problem solve the equations around me;

And my society.

I don't want to feel insecurities;

But feel immortality and finish off my problems I have with fatality.

Many people tell me I have different personalities;

All I'm doing is getting with reality.

But I want to express my feelings psychologically and
have many skills that were built on sociology.

The tears that were shed in my life; my apologies.

But in my life it was based on technicalities.

But at last and finally I found some spirituality and
morality this is my life as if we are living in zoology.

This is how it all started back in the 11th grade at Mayfield High School. Leading up to this very moment in my life; to writing this book of poems.

When I was in Mrs. Lynn Connelly's speech class, she caused me to have a breakthrough in my life. She taught me how to express myself more efficiently by teaching me to understand poetry and analyze it.

Now I give all of this back by saying thank you to my
speech teacher and those of you who have supported me
in my life's journey by reading about "My Life".
As you read my other poems you will understand a
different Raw, creativity, and the deep thoughts of my
intellectual side that was never brought to the public.

I hope you all embrace what I have to say and love it. Enjoy!!!

Mother's Day

Today we come together to celebrate and
Dedicate this special cause for mother's day.
We the youth and men want to say happy
mother's day. Even though that's not
enough to say. We the men of Glenville
SDA wants to say it anyway. This mother's
day should be honor in a spiritually way
and in an appreciative way.
Mother's day should be celebrated in a
creative way. Mothers should be known
for their hospitality and having their kids
see reality. The mothers did their part in
giving us birth it was a blessing never a curse.
As boys and girls get older mothers will
always be at their kids shoulders.

Devastation

In this world we all go through devastation.

It's throughout our entire nation.

The struggles that come and go in our lives is a form
of fragmentation thats deep within our hearts.

There has been proof shown by demonstration of
discrimination that we all are facing.

We shouldn't use isolation against devastation.

Let's not focus on so much video games; like
PlayStation and focus more on our education.

Once we get through the trials and tribulations we
can all come together as one congregation.

But the people in the world become of the world so they use negotiation
against each other like they're going through discombobulation.

The things that we do that's dangerous is an act of transgression.

But what do we know?

Our mind aren't focus; it's playing tricks on us like we
in a world of triangulation and desertification.

If we put our minds to it we can do it;

Like fight the evils that lurks within the earth
by collaboration and determination.
Also we shouldn't use each other as subrogation.

But without the conflictions we go through like frustrations
lack of communication causes us to have limitations.

So we should rise-up and speak-up;

Not against each other with hostile language in a different translation.

We should be more supportive of people's ideas and not take
them for grant it like they're criminals of their circumstances.

We the people of the world should be able to meet
and greet each other by saying congratulations not
use false accusations now that's devastation.

BLM

Can You See Within Me

I'm a black statistic.
The words that come out my mouth will have you twisted.
And say I'm sorry I missed it.
I'm drifting away from all my problems I can't even solve them.
Because I'm stuck in a black cloudy hole which is
controlling my mind, body and inner soul.

It seems that I can't grasp the cold.
I been told the world isn't all that cruel and cold.
The world holds the key to success and God
has many tests, for us to go through.
And pursue our own lifestyles and destines too.
So listen to my poem deeply.
Because clearly I can't see within me.

I want to resolve this silent pause inside of me.
Because my anger is what you can see.
But it's not within me.
On top of it all I want to stand tall.
I never want to fall.
Or don't have a destination so instead I hit a brick wall.
I want to let go of all my flaws and take
control of all my morals and cause.

God made 10 simple for us to follow.
It's time for me to come out of the shadows.
And stay in Gods battle.
To survive and rise from all evil lies.
Above all I been through I don't want to be a
disappointment to my fellow people.
And my community too.

Temptation

Is it true what they say about temptation?
It's like you being sucked into a gravitational pull.
That puts you in a situation of lust.
Not knowing what comes next but believing in
something you and I both trust in.

It's a high point we youth are facing into today's
society with our raging sexual urges.
And uncontrollable hormone balance.
It's a challenge.
For us you see.
It's like a high "a sensational high" that lies within us and the impurities.
Instead we just caught up in sin catching any
known to man sexual transmitted diseases.
(STD's) like H.I.V....
Does it drive us this far too loose our virginity?
Yes!
Or is it a cry out for unity?
Maybe!
We the worldly people should have temptation in a good
way like in a spiritual way or harmonizing way.
We should wait until that time for marriage not
miss use our-selves for a miss carriage.

The innocents we choose to loose.
Shows us that Jesus is coming back very soon.
The music we listen to will come to a complete
hault so we should stay in tune.
Not think about the impure thoughts of this unclean world.
The youth and elderly should take a real close look at Love.
Trust, Sex, and see what it is really all about.
It seems as though we would do anything for temptation.
What's that about?

BLM

Why Am I A Lame?
C.S.S.

Why Am I A Lame?
It's because yesterday's news became my reality
and living up to my mentality.
Choosing my games I play into today's society.
And living into the video games physiologically.

Then thinking to dress to impress for that one person
you thought was special but became trouble.
Have me realize all the times we spent together was all lies.
And didn't want to even fall back because.

I fell into so many peoples traps.
Then feeling like I have gotten smacked.
Which is whack.

This time I'm no longer going to put myself out there into the wilderness.
It's my own personal quest.
As also my request.

I don't want to be judged on the good fellowship I bring to the
table, not being in the same situation of Kane and Able.
I'm trying to wave all odds that has been pointed at me of being a lame.
It's like me being nameless just because I'm different.
All I have to say to any and everybody that call people
lames because of their lack of dissatisfaction of them.
Is that you became lames because all of you are jealous of me.
Mad and think you all are bad because you all want to be me.
Really you all.
"Can't See Me".

You people are screwed up because I finally
beat y'all at y'all own games for once.
You all misinterpret me and clearly misjudged me.
I'm just giving y'all the facts.
I'm back here lies Branford Lewis Moton beating
the odds of being a lame or being nameless.

So don't be mad at me.
Read Proverbs 3:5-6 KJV Trust in the Lord with all thine
heart; and lean not unto thine own understanding. In all thy
ways acknowledge him, and he shall direct thy paths.
But be a witness of not being a lame.
Pay attention don't be a statistic of being a lame.
You all have a name.

As I look back on this poem and my emotions that I put into it; it seems
kind of funny to me that I came up with the title "Why Am I Lame"?
Back in elementary school to high school, even
somewhat now; I felt as though I never fit in.
The people who knew me or know of me look at me like I'm a lame.
It made me feel as though I had to press through the
issues by writing and venting out this deep pain.
I kept these things hidden within me. So I decided to tell
the world; including the people who feel or felt like me or
is going through the same things that I went through.
This is not to discourage but encourage those who have been subjected
to or victimized by the thoughts of not being what people want you to be.
So to shed light I want you to know this one fact; you can
be whoever you want to be; just have confidence in yourself
and know that nobody can take that away from you.
Remember; you are worth more than what people say you are; don't pay
any attention to what they say. But be encouraged; my fellow readers.

BLM

No More Sob Stories

Sob Stories!
A story you should never forget.
I must fret.
This story I shall not and will not ever regret.
I'm tired of the hurt and pain it drives me insane.
To my everyday working brain.

I think my emotional problems came & went to
never realizing to even saying I apologize.
And to sympathize.
With all the people who tell me how they were mesmerized.
On their own sob stories.
When I hear sob stories it lashes at me like a hard shock to the body.

It rains but it pours.
Hearing such sad stories.
I want to be set free from them not run.
But if it helps to hear another person's sob story.
Instead of picking up a loaded gun.
Then they win.
I'm all up for grabs.
But I will always and never forget that same or
different sob story people will tell me.

Hoping that I didn't fail you see;
Because me;
I want to be;
A person who won't let anybody down;
And them looking upon me;
With a sob story frown.

BLM
2008 It's Time to CELEBRATE

I Thought About

What I thought about?
I came to realize I already knew about.
You wonder why I say that?
It's because when I was a child I spoke as a child,
I thought as a child, I walked as a child.
Back then I didn't know any better and now I do.
Because I found a way out by becoming a
man putting away childish things.

People didn't know what I was capable of.
And thought I was played out.
This is my way of saying this is how I came about.
To think about the American Dream people never heard or knew about.
All people can say is what about.
But it's time to make a change.
I'm not going to keep on depending on.
My Life, Devastation, Can You See Within Me,
TEMPTATION, WANTING TO BE WANTED, Counting
On My Blessings, and Why Am I A Lame?
I'm beyond that.
I can overcome what I thought about instead I can
show people what I was taught about.

BLM
2008 It's Time to CELEBRATE

Family Issues

What do I mean exactly when I say family issues?
Listen up because I'm going to tell you.
Family issues are questions and answers that you
will never know or receive because.
There are problems, questions, and answers
that you or your family can't solve.

But all you can do is be the cause.
Or the person that's involved.
In the family ties and lies.
Family now a days don't stick to what they say or going to do.
It's basically up to you to choose.
What you are going to do and pursue.
It's just like they say the world can either make you or break you.

But really they're saying look around you boy/
girl or man & woman get a clue fool.
This takes me back to what I was saying about family.
All family is good for is money sometimes and unsolved
questions & answers not asked for advice.

Despite what they say or do to you.
It's up to you to show yourself approve or improve.
Even when you are in a bad ass mood.
They're going to either ask "what's wrong" or say it's going to be okay".
Anyway back to what I was saying.
My family seems to not show any remorse.
Or any kind of sympathy of course.
It's like they want you to walk in the storm all
alone and try to make it on your own.

No Ring a Ding Ding from your family to see if you're okay at home.
If they do call it's only to the people they play favorites to.
Or like despite if they are your close relative.

My only option is to separate and make my life positive
and stay away from family members that's negative.

To think all these years what the family been through too.
My family really hasn't changed.
Even the holidays and going to church don't seem to be the same.
They smile and laugh in front of your face but they
probably thinking get this Negro up out of my face.
Before I catch a case.

But really there is enough said than done already because.
We still didn't get to the bottom of my family issues.
Accept all the bad things to look forward to.
It's okay though.
Because no matter what.
There is still going to be disputes in family issues.

Well we all have been there and done that;
Meaning family issues being the cause or the victim of a no win
solution. Of course there's not a good or bad person in the family but
there are unresolved issues and situations. The reason for this poem
is to deal with life situations with family. Because I personally dealt
with it in my own life and also witnessed it in other people lives.

I feel that family is important and people that go through
various drama filled spats aren't the only ones. We all have
stories to tell; I just needed to vent that out because we all know
that most people go through drama with their families.
We also know that families don't always get along. Sometimes we share
good moments and even laugh at each other's pain like Kevin Hart.

BLM
2008 It's Time to CELEBRATE

Wanting To Be Wanted!!!!
C.S.S.

I feel like I'm dehydrated and frustrated from being unwanted.
People that once loved or love me.
Put me in a position of feeling like I'm on America's Most Wanted.
I was taught that I shouldn't care about what others think of me.
I have a mind of my own and I don't want to
roam or die in this world all alone.

It's hard to feel wanted if people don't check up on you or invite you in.
It's not only a crime known to man.
It's also a sin.
This pain that's within me is hurting me inside.
It needs to be exposed.
I don't want people looking at me as a lost hopeless soul.
Like I'm on trial in front of a judge saying case closed.

But I don't want that to happen.
Because I feel like my feelings is being
pushed back behind closed doors.
I don't want this to continue on like rumors turning into wars.
I guess I found some of the answers I've been looking for.
Instead of feeling down and poor.
Or even unwanted....

At this starting point of my life not really excelling or progressing
in my poetry or having much more life experiences.
But just being down on life and not really feeling
like I had a shoulder to lean on or cry on.
Just wishing that I would have dealt with the situations
in my life better or talking to someone about it.

But this is a story for each individual who or whom will read this. Who
have felt alone at their most vulnerable moments in life to needing
a hug or shoulder to cry on? Because this is a poem for it to being
understanding that you weren't alone and I too felt this way and went
on in my teenage years. To going through those life changing phases.

To realizing the world isn't that bad just to take life as
it comes or better yet "grab life by the horns".

Committed

Determined to stick with it.
No matter what comes my way or what I face.
I'm going to give everybody a taste of my face.
And what I was focus on.
Whether I was right or wrong.
Being committed is your own personification
not turning it into a situation.

Taking the time.
To not spend a dime and having that security in your own personality.
Having a dream whether it's big or small.
You are taking charge to stand tall.

To commit to something.
You are implicating that you aren't going to show any failure.
But show good pleasure and purpose.
Showing that you're not worthless.
To amount to nothing but it's turning it into
something isn't being committed.

My commitment.
Is to stay committed.
Even when I'm really not focused on it.
I realize in my past even now that the only way to thrive.
You have to learn how to drive.
Maybe that's just it.
Me being committed.
And being above the odds of failure.
Committed.

BLM
2008 It's Time to CELEBRATE

My Fate

My fate is on the line.
Lights, cameras, action it's about time.
For my fate not to be taken into my own hands.
But into God's hands.
No not right now.
I'm not a big fan of God.
But I really do want to be.
Because like I said my fate is on the line.

I may not be trying as I ought to be.
But I want to be.
Relieved of stress and be set free and bless.
Yes I'm down in the dumps of my mistakes.
I guess this was a wake up call.
For me to rise up on my feet and stand tall.
But really I've been afraid of change.
And growing up.

But society doesn't really care about that.
This is about time for me to walk the walk and
talk the talk and put it into action.
Instead of sitting down and relaxing.
My fate doesn't include me to have so many down falls.
And don't take higher standard shots in the harsh world.
It's not time to escape from me becoming successful and great.
I'm descant to be great.
It's my fate.
No I don't have all the time in the world to get myself together.
But I know one thing it's not going to take me forever to do it.

So all I have to remember is.
If I let God apart of my life.
I can do it if I put my mind to it.
Instead of living polluted.
And just losing it.
I mean all I have.
After all it's my fate to inspire someone else to be successful and great.

BLM
2008 It's Time to CELEBRATE

Floetry
C.S.S.

The rhymes I put together feel so clever.
And seems like it will last forever.
Although this poem is so much more it's my flow to my floetry.
I like making people feel intuned like iTunes so to speak.
To such a pretty or beautiful word as poetry.
I would like for people to notice me.
Or even acknowledge me.
When they read or see my poetry.

I would like to consider myself as a creative artiste
when it comes to creative writing or you can call me the
old R &B musical group Jodeci to my floetry.
I have a deep connection of my expression to poetry.
It's my love of poetry that soothes me.
It's my message.
Like a text message it's instant it just comes to me.

My floetry is authentic.
It keeps you well grounded as it's visibly printed.
Every word I spit or read I meant it.
Because things I think of I can twist it like.
What goes up must come down.
Or you can take me on another round.
That's what I do after all I'm twisted, energetic, sophisticated,
and poetic and some people already know it to.

This poem is expressing more of my creativity. To making simple
analogies and metaphors. So clever and unique to bringing out
the inner glow within me. With coming up with a poem called
"Floetry" it is like a flow to me, as if you see people rapping,
oppose to free -styling your words on paper or out loud.

BLM
2009s FINEST

Earthquakes

There are so many natural causes of mother nature
disasters that happens all around the world.
But there's one that stands out to me and that is "Earthquakes".
You can't stop it or escape it or even prevent it from happening.

It's like you're trapped in a life or death situation when it can
happen in any location at any time or moment of the day.
Many people has died or lived through it to
tell their life experiences of it.

What most people don't know is the causes of it.
The reason for the cause is there's platelets called
Tectonic Plates on the earths crust.
Below the ocean sea floor that shifts up & down
that affects the impact of the ocean.
This strikes a heavy motion on the earth's surface of the ocean.

In simpler terms part of the earthquake is like shaking
up a snow globe which would feel like part of the earth
just folded and been reshaped and molded.
You have been duly noted on how earthquakes can cause
trauma for many people even for thee economy.

So we have to be safe and aware because just wakening
up or walking out the door is a big scare.

BLM
2009s FINEST

K.I.N.G. of POP

R.I.P. MICHAEL Jackson
August 29, 1958, - June 25, 2009

He could sing.
He could dance.
Lastly but not least he was a perfectionist.
He's Michael Jackson!!!

The King of Pop just dropped dead from
millions of fans of a cardiac-arrest.
Now he's at rest because there is no longer a heart beat in his CHEST.
It's been shocking and extreme to Michael Jackson's
up random and unexpected DEATH.

People thought he was an idol or icon even a ladies man.
He was a musical genius and sensational dancer and a musical planner.
MJ was unbelievable as he would say "UNBELIEVABLE!"
We will all miss this legendary musical soul of pop icon.
He was smooth and slick like a python.

The way I sit here and write this smooth but cool wicked rhyme.
Michael could do it better 10xs.
Although MJ was in his PRIME TIME.
Which won't be forgotten or left behind.
You will be missed like a special first kiss.
Your music will live on through many artists and many of your memories.
Even the highs, the lows and breeze that runs through the trees.
You gave us something to achieve and believe in.
Although this isn't a goodbye.

This just a rebirth of you staying alive in our hearts and minds.
But as you would say it's hard to say goodbye
But it's human nature.
You will be remembered forever and live on in our hearts and minds.
Rest in Peace Michael Jackson.

R.I.P.

MJ

BLM
2009s FINEST

Count Your Blessings

I'm 18 and already haven't experience life through God's eyes.
It seems that the blessings that I did count were all lies.
I didn't mean it and didn't believe in it.
My prayers became into wants.
Not asking for help to answer my prayers.

I guess I'm taking the time to ask God to hear me out and forgive me.
My cries have turned into tears.
I don't want to lose the blessings that were stored upon me.
And to live in fear a and don't stop to think to even care.

I want the Holy Spirit apart of my life.
Not go through pain and strife.
Instead maybe I can be a witness to God to save a life.
Because at the end Jesus will forgive me for my sins.
If I don't get my blessings right now.
It will probably fall on death ears.
So it will be no blessings to count it will all disappear.

BLM
2009s FINEST

One Step At A Time

I wake up early every morning.
Taking one step at a time.
As I climb out my bed I try to stay in my right faith and frame of mind.
Throughout the day I take that extra step to
stay focus and be on my grind.

But it's hard because I haven't been true to myself or kind.
I can't help but to think about the past, my present, and the future.
It's holding me back.
My only choice is to stay where I'm at.
And watch what I lack.

One step at a time.
Take a deep breathe 1&, 2&, 3&, 4 and breathe.
My troubles have just begun.
I'm having mixed emotions and not going through
my brain's pulse or body's motion.
Losing all hope on life because of my past life of what I had.
I was depressed and little bit still am but I was glad.
Of what I had back at home.
But I can't let that stop me I have to keep moving on and be strong.

One step at a time!
I guess this is a moving stepping point in my life to let go and move on.
I haven't lived long or as strong but did a lot of
wrong and wanting to repent for it.
I have to find away to make everything I do or even say to be okay.

Every day is a special day for me.
And anyone else who believes.
To wanting to achieve.
Is a good belief and one step ahead of taking one step at a time.
I haven't reached my prime.
And I'm not ready but when I am ready it will be time.

So as long as I live and breathe every day and moment I live.
I'm going to take this slow, steady, peacefully.
And every day one step at a time as long as I'm on the right path.
And on time.
Me taking one step at a time.

BLM
2009s FINEST

I Let My Pencil Do The Talking

Have I.
This 21 year old guy.
Experience the true meaning of writing a rhyme?
Even letting the lead of the pencil taste the paper as I savor my words.
In a burst of excitement like eating a starburst
as I splurge on my words on paper.

So listen to me closely.
Because I don't bite down on my words.
I let my pencil do the talking.
While I do the walking.
I do encourage to write down descriptive words like pronouns and verbs.
And countless of meaningful words.

To get my point across.
Because I'm lost and a mind is a terrible thing to waste
and don't have me spitted out like toothpaste.
As I look at the world in the face.
So I can concentrate onto my poetic place.
And let the knowledge come back to me like the
song "Back to life back to reality".

But all I can say.
I'm focus on my individuality.
Like earth on gravity.
To believe in this poem like my words I hide in my dome.
To take this poem.
To ultimate heights.
Of being great because my mind is in flight.
And "I am so bright".
This infinite gift I have can be ricocheted to wisdom and
words of math stirring you onto the right path.
And people don't laugh.
Because I'm on a whole another level beyond thee beyond.
You can refer this poem on or off the richterscale.

Because of the magnitude of energy you will
receive or breathe in from this poem.
My pencil will have you reap what you've sown.
Because I silence you to a tombstone.
And I'm on top like a king of his throne.
Because I'm "So Far Gone" like Drake.
When he speak so vividly in his raps.

I say it as I quote it.
Because my pencil wrote it.
It's like I surpass my penmanship on the tip of my tongue.
That can't say too much when I have my
pencil on the tips of my fingertips.
My pencil has my mouth on mute or zipped.

Because it don't want to release too much info by my
vociferous words that has been thrown out the window.
To my pencil it's alive & well that has been taken over by my
mind and body like a movie that has been voice-over as well.
My pencil has taken over and prevailed.
I let my pencil do the talking while my words and I do the walking.

BLM
2010 ALL I DO IS WIN

Nothing Has Changed

It's a brand new year and nothing has changed.
The game remains the same.
But no change.
How people gone change.
For the lime light or for the fame.
When really they can't stay true to the game.
People are acting like some true lames.
And differently when each year should be a lesson learned not a waste.
What's the point of a "New Years Resolution?"
When all people is doing is being the
POLLUTION of a no win SOLUTION.

I'm disappointed in America.
But mainly the people of America.
I know it may take some time to see a change.
Like when we voted for OBAMA.
But like Tupac said "It's time to make a Change".
Guess what y'all people of the United States or Nation which ever.
I don't write for the fame or pretend like I know the earth.
And place it as a game.

I do it because I make my way through it.
Or to keep my sanity.
When really what people is doing to me is killing me.
Or each other for that matter.
My belief and convictions are like a pancake batter.
Ready to be shaped and molded into something better.
Well that's how I look at America waiting for something good
to happen or better yet for an inspirational change.

Just maybe I'm probably waiting on myself to change.
But to be real with y'all.
I saw and know it's going to be a change.
Because I'm going to be true and real to the game.
As long as my name is Branford Lewis Moton I have essentially spoken.

It's still going to remain the same.
Like the phrase "Nothing Has Changed".
It's a new GAME this season.
And I'm not talking about the audio video.
I'm talking about the show.
That's why I'm looking forward to this year to pop off like
an explosion which has taken place in the show.
Because I feel this year have already taken off into a bombshell.
To be prepared for the worse and prevailed on and off the richterscale.

My change is progress or processed like a
transferrable agreement through a computer.
Still active not so much in work.
But for this year and every year after.
I'm the man that has a plan ready to put in some work.
I'm not going to slack off.
And be that dude on the street with nothing to eat.

That has nothing to show for himself or America.
All I can say out the mouth or other people see and say
nothing has changed but people manage to be the same.
As the game does not change.
But still nothing has changed.

BLM
2011 THE SKIES THE LIMIT

Collaboration
C.S.S.

Introducing one of kind.
Meet two of kind because my cousin and I spit
one of two of the opposite rhymes.
You can call it "The Great American Past Time".
This collaboration is my admiration to both of the world's
twisted so sick with it surgically a match in imagination.
Translation my cousin Bartholomew Creighton Moorman
and Branford Lewis Motion is two peas and pod.
You will find us quite odd.

Which the world don't know what they've done.
They release two of the deadliest most powerful sons.
Of the city of Cleveland.
We've been Cleveland's favorite ultimate dual so who knows.
You may get a combination is my destination to throw people off track.
Like T-Wayne better known as T-Pain & Lil Wayne a creative match.
When we come hard that means we go hard.
Like T-Pain & Kayne West and leave the mark of the beast on your chest.

No second chance or but my first impression.
Teaching these young adults and adolescence.
It's a sensational pain running through our veins.
To the crowd of the fans.
Looking at the sky promising God don't let us give up until the end.
Changing one nation at a time like we Jehovah
Witnesses because people need to witness this.
"The history in the making".
We taken over like God's army vs Satin.
This is my deep conversation.
Like I was in deep penetration.
With the word conjugation.
Twisted up like Nikki Minaj & Eminem.
My Roman's empire to my cousin & I Roman's revenge.

I'm not done yet with my binge.
But I forgot to tell you all this.
It's just my introduction.
Throwing out my repercussions and preventing
myself from cussing out the mouth.
No I wasn't born and raised from the south.
My mom was.
Growing up without a biological dad in the home.
Feeling so sensitive and alone born into a broken home.
Prone to doing so much wrong.
Look you all I'm foaming from the mouth to pouring
out so much anguish and pain from the heart.
I should have been dealing with this better from the start.

Detonation its over.
Precipitation don't care whether the weather gets better.
I'm never gettin better.
People say never say never.
I'm a lever.

Always gettin pulled in the mix.
I'm fixated.
My life's complicated.
The black sheep of a herd.
An abomination of this world.
Treated like a girl.
Homosexuality makes me hurl.

I'm the root of my own problem.
Holdin myself back from the world.
Afraid of the light I hide in the dark.
Don't even know myself.
Let alone my own name.

So how can I be that lil boy from the Simpsons.
How can I live.
Growin up to be someone I hated.
If trials and tribulations is the question.
Is a bullet the answer.
If my pain was smoke I would've died 10 years ago of cancer.

Askin Jesus for the answers.
And Jesus is so confused he ask God for the answers.
I'm a stranger to myself.
Elaborating with determination.
Infactuations with realization.

I'm God's son an odd son.
Angry inside.
No one helpin to figure out solutions.
I'm shootin poison.
The food I eat, the girls I lay with corruption I dream about.
School I hated.
If I overcome my struggles I adominated.
This is my Mexico.
My life's stretch.
I take my day like a journey a single step at a time.

Rhyme after rhyme.
Tryin to take over my life's order.
Turnin a dime into a quarter.
Hurtin since the elementary.
Not tryin to end up in the penitentiary.

One day I want to be a part of black history.
This is my legacy.
Thinkin if I will ever see.
A junior.
My metaphors are recipies for tumors.

My memories are contusions.
I lost points.
I'm losing my grade score.
I'm the eighth darf.
I'm my family's black sheep.
My cousin has his innocence.
Lost mine between junior high and high school.
Did so much dirt lost track my clothes are dirty.
Not sure if I'm gonna make it to the age of thirty.

My life is my life it was crappy.
Just hopin I will wake up and this was just my imagination.
Hopes gone welcome to Branford and Bart's collaboration.

This is the very first poem that my cousin and I both created
and collaborated on and it's also one of my favorites.
It amazes me how my cousin put so much raw, energetic,
feelings into this poem; especially how he ended it. Then
how I started and ended; so he can start his part.
The whole making of this poem project was so creative and inventive
that we could actually see how it could go viral, turning into a small fire,
then into a wild fire and then ultimately blossoming into a wild flower.
I know I was being too descriptive on the details of getting
my point across; but this is such a great creation.
I'm glad we went forth with this great creation. I wouldn't give this
moment up for anything; because this is a great moment for me.
To be able to write something with my cousin so meaningful,
and also having the ability to capture something so
precious in writing form; is AWESOME!
This is for you Bart. I thank you for being a cousin, brother, friend
and confidant. Thank you for being a part of this project and pushing
my vocabulary to new lengths and depths, also I couldn't have
done this without you; just want you to know I appreciate you.

BLM & BCM
2011 THE SKIES THE LIMIT

Dead Wrong

I never say the right thing so it always comes out wrong.
Put me on Biggie's documentary call me dead wrong like the song.

I don't own up to my rights but live up to my wrongs.
See that didn't make sense like this poem "Dead Wrong".
Look at Sean Puffy Combs living up life and did Biggie Smalls so wrong.

Which in this case he's dead wrong.
Look at a snake they even shed wrong.
What happen to Tupac Shakur found dead outside a casino
that Suge Knight may or may not be linked to.
Listen to the words I'm speaking to you.
Dead Wrong.
Times are wasting.
People coming up missing.
A new start of the investigation.
And the end of migration.
Dead presidents faces are deteriorating.
Having people in the Republican office hating.
On the Democratic party.
Because they don't care about our lives and the cause.
Is they living life like it's a party.

Every scenario I brought up has caught up with me.
To being the questions and answers of being dead wrong.
Ding dong.
I'm not trying to be a dead wrong prestidigitator.
But that dude has his head on Inspirator see you later alligator.
I'm not trying to be a dead wrong fabricator.
A dead man at his thrown.
Who's DEAD WRONG.
A ding dong.
I'm King Kong.
I been wrong.
Hate my voice.

Can't sing a song.
Break my toys.
A boy to a man.
Too much noise.

I know I can.
Its nasty.
Drop the t y.
I'm fly.
Not a regular guy.
Been through hell and back.
Ended up between Earth and Hell.
Two of the same.
My dreams burnin up in flames.
I only want to survive.
All about me is a lie.
A mammal with a bone.
Sleepin incognito with stones.
Left alone with nobody.
I'm a nobody.
Got no logic.
I'm a product of this universe society variety of idiocy.
Open the curtains.
So u can see its me.
I'm home alone.
I'm dead wrong.

BCM & BLM
2011 THE SKIED THE LIMIT

Mentally Challenged

I'm mentally challenged.
Visibly speaking.
Physically challenged.
To reaching the impossible.
Invisibly challenged.
Or better yet challenged.
At being the best in the poetry game.
So far gone to Barack Obama's change.
Is reaching to the top challenge of the lyrical hip-hop food chain.

Take a pause.
Or a moment of silence.
So I can reboot or restart my thought process up again.
My brain wave is up again.
Getting into the game Brain Age I'm up for to win.
Brain clouded once again time to reup my thought
process like we breathe in oxygen.
There I go speaking in tongues fumbling on the words I come upon.

Storing all of my creativity in my brain in all good fun.
I am that chosen son.
To think about all the things I can't come across.
Because my mind is filled with confusion
and my derailed train of thought.
But yet when people belittle me.
Or my intelligence that my creative writing
explain it's self which makes it relevant.
No I'm not the brightest.
But I do have the midst touch.
I don't need no good luck.

Taking on surgery like the show Nip Tuck.
Needless to say I am breathing or even seeing.
Salutations to my mentally challenged unbalanced brain's graduation.
It's been a long time coming vacation.
To completing the next chapter to my destination.

Times are wasting.
Sitting on my bed contemplating.
On the challenges that I'm facing.
Especially to my mentally challenged brain.
Yes I have the common sense to keep sane.
But I'm going to keep giving people a piece of my brain.
As long as it doesn't rain.
A mentally challenged brain.

The reason for this poem "Mentally Challenged" is I find myself going
through a lot of issues and problems in my day to day life. Issues that
I face in the real world or just academically in school, and at home;
to caring about what people say and think of me; myself included.
When you don't believe in yourself or your work ethics you begin
to feel a certain way about it; like doubting your confidences,
wondering if you're good enough. But mainly it's to prove yourself
wrong, everyone else who doubted you and sometimes just to
uplift yourself by being and doing my best, by venting out built up
feelings; to just being a pure genius in this creative poetry society.

I hope when you all read this you understood the message
I was writing to get a better understanding of me. The
what, how, and why I wrote this particular poem.

BLM
2011 THE SKIES THE LIMIT

Imagination

It's funny.
Thinking of the next best thing of my wonderous brain.
Which can be a pain.
At times.
But it is my imagination.
Which gives me the thrive for greatness and good writing conversation.
To thinking.
What was so funny in the first place.
Of having creative imagination.

It's amazing.
So amazing.
That I'm creating ideas for my art work that's in work.
To performing the art of lyricism.
To expressing the word of art of lyricism.
In a poetic sense.
All I can do is imagine every new word I learn.
Then turn it into visual aid on paper like a presentation.
Just like my imagination.

Let me just kick it old school for you.
Real old school like the Temptations.
"It was just my imagination running away with me".
It was just my imagination running away with me.
Now I created art with two punch-lines.
Then savoring the punch-lines.
As I savor a bunch of punch-lines of rhymes.

Just call me Rhyme Fest.
Taking off my bulletproof vest.
Giving you nothing more and nothing less.
But giving you more of my best.
And less of my stress.
Giving you taste what's on my mind.
Not portraying my zodiac sign.
You have to be on an intellectual's grind.
Than knowing the transparent mind.

But being in my head for just a day is seeing everything okay.
It's like any and everything is extraordinaire.
You can see things so crystal clear.
After all is said and done.
My vision to my imagination is ever so clear like outer space-atmosphere.
So stop and stare like the band One Republic.
Because I'm giving you a demonstration of my imagination.
To the public.
And people is going to love it.
So what of it this is my transformation.
Better yet call it my imagination.

BLM
2011 THE SKIES THE LIMIT

Over Load

Corruption
Corruption
system malfunction
System has over load
Over load

I have a lot on my plate.
Which has me speaking like a computerize robot.
I've dropped my ex-gf.
And been on the spot ever since.
My mom and I relationship doesn't even make sense.

I spent the last 3 years.
To not a accomplishing anything.
To overcoming an over load of problems can't top
overwhelming situations or even solve them.
I feel like I'm at a malpractice.
With mine and everyone else who include
me in their issues and situations.

No one can't understand my over load.
Or my linguistic.
Oops I'm sorry you missed it my language.
My head is ready to explode.
I repeat.
Almost at maximum over load.
So much to think about.
Repress in with doubt trying to find a way out.
Life decisions being dragged in the mixed with unreasonable doubt.
I want to be at peace and say peace out sorry doubt.
I want to count on God not depend on myself alone.
Because at the end of the day your all alone.

But at this point I'm going back and fourth with
a critical life decision or decisions.
Asking and waiting on God's permission to
show me as a man my life's lesson.
As I go through life & press on with my progression.

I want to impact this world with my writing poetry.
As my legacy.
To completing the ultimate challenge overloading
too many downloads of life problems.
I finally reached that altitude in life not being high on life.
But down on life to realizing what I have to do not be that loose screw.
That doesn't support the surface of the floor board right.
But learning each year as a man to dealing
with life or eventful destructions.
My own corruptions.
Me just being overboard.
As to being an overload..
I officially have 10 seconds;
10, 9, 8, 7, 6, 5, 4, 3, 2, 1
SYSTEM HAS O-V-E-R-L-O-A-D.

BLM
2011 THE SKIES THE LIMIT

Radiant Beauty

Your radiant beauty has me mesmerized.
I see through the sex and focus on your pretty brown eyes.
Instead of what lies between your thighs.
If I made a mistake of coming onto strong.
I apologize.

When we text and talk on the phone.
I consider you to be one of the guys.
This is the truth that lies within my pride.
But I'm a poet sent from God to tell you what's real or odd.
Yeah I can be sincere the man of the year.
But let's switch gears.
You that woman of the year.
You have my mind blown.
To a different planet.
Because I have no reason and I can't stand it.

But I do have a reason.
It's for me to get to know you as my friend.
And not play pretend.
Let's begin again.
Your radiant beauty has me mesmerized.
I see through the sex and focus on your pretty brown eyes.
Instead of what lies between your inner thighs.

I know you seen and heard this before.
But I'm not like all the other guys.
And that's the truth that's no lie.
You're crazy, sexy, cool, and the words that roll off the tip of your tongue.
Is so smooth
oooh!
you're so cool!

Yes you now have a beautiful baby and she's going
to grow up a beautiful intelligent young lady.
Just like her mommy oooh you're so fine and kind.
This poem can last forever as if I was Keith Sweat.
Making it last forever.
Because this poem is more like a romance movie or novel.

This is me on the gravel talking about that
glorious battle me in the shadows.
Of her radiant beauty.
Beaming down on me like a sun ray.
But hey I'm not going to forget that beautiful day.

When I saw her radiant beauty in my way.
Her radiant beauty isn't like a fantasy love movie it's more like true TV.
So please don't judge me.
I'm just trying to be real.
And showing you what the deal.
Is of telling you how I feel.
Your radiant beauty has me mesmerized.
I see through the sex and focus on your pretty brown eyes
instead of what lies between your inner thighs.
Sincerely radiant beauty of God.

BLM
2011 THE SKIES THE LIMIT

It's Show Time

Thank you
Thank you
Thank you
You all have been so kind.
And wonderful audience.
I must make my closing performance so let's get to it.

It's show time you all.
This is me standing tall.
To the open mic.
I didn't just pick up the pencil and paper to become a poet overnight.
The words I speak to you tonight.
Is in bright lights.
It's plain and simple.
As I bust out with an innovative poetic speech like a pimple.

I will have you all in your seats.
Move to the beat.
Like a cymbal.
Please you all hold onto your applause and don't tremble from your seats.
Because this poem is a groove.
So get it up and move to your feet.
My inspiring words don't move single individuals
it moves the people of the streets.

I'm unknown being introduced to being well known.
As long as I'm on top of my (A) game.
I'm not walking away from my thrown.
So please quiet down and turn down or off all electronic devices.
As they are my distractions.
I'm giving you the best part of me; my interactions.
Yeah I know I'm no Michael Jackson.
But I'm something more the main attraction.

Can the show continue on?
Or should I end it as of now?
Like "Over" the song.
Am I wrong for being real.
Going straight for the kill verbally as people
just curse me and my talent?
As the saying goes; a mind is terrible thing to waste.
Well it's also tragic.

While I end tonight's show with my reconciliation.
I'm going out with a bang no chains involved.
But me going out with no doubt but round for
round, pound for pound of rhymes.
Yeah I call that lights out.
There's no more wasting yours or my time.
Now what you call that SHOW TIME.

BLM
2011 THE SKIES THE LIMIT

Over
C.S.S.

When it's all said and done everything changes until it's all over.
Allow me to introduce myself "BLM" Branford Lewis Motion.
Yup that's me and yes I am speaking.
No wait I have spoken.
No this is me joking.

This isn't no Nintendo.
I'm no game token.
But no worries my feeling weren't hurt nor did
I put my feelings into too much.pain.
Shattered dreams as to my screams.
Is to my nightmares.

Girls come and go out my life.
A big world affair.
Nowhere to turn.
My heart burns.
But can I do what Usher did!
"Let it Burn"
Or should I do what Lil Wayne and Eminem did pick up the
world and drop it on someone's head or just drop dead.
So it can be all over.
My rage is at supernova.
I'm going through the motion.
I have no more emotion.
I'm drained this isn't no life gain all I can feel or see is pain.

The words I use to combine has intertwined.
No this is me going over the deep end.
Going life blind.
Running out of life's time.
Only time can tell.
When it rains.
You know there's a HELL.
I'm tearing up the richterscale.
Whether I'm on or off the weighing scale.
I'm done I went towards the molten lava hot SUN.
It's over you tell me?
Have I really won?

The reason for this poem being called "Over" because I was going through a lot of things in my life. I was feeling like no one really understood me or was helping me through the situations. So i felt the need to vent out and let loose everything and just give a little of my all with my rage and pain included.

To keep me from going inasane to keep my sanity.
So those of you who know me; you have all witnessed my pain and rage. So I hope everyone get the just of what I was going through, and not misinterpret what you don't hear or look into. But just grasp the sense of what i was trying to make sense of in this poem.

BLM
2011 THE SKIES THE LIMIT

Explode
C.S.S.

KABOOM
KABOOM KABOOM; explosion ahead.
My rage is like a locked up, cage animal.
To not knowing what I'm capable of.
To not being true to myself or showing no love.
No hugs or kisses.
But danger anger as to people dismisses.

Many hopeful wishes to clinch my skin of angry pinches.
Needing attention for a cure because I'm not following
the heart of Jesus because my heart isn't pure.
No longer can I endure this cure.
Because I'm not feeling secure.
Is my anger.
As to a stranger.
Meaning me the other half of my behalf?
To becoming an emotional melt down of destructions.
Many of my unidentified corruptions.

No this isn't me bluffing.
But this is me puffing out the steam within myself esteem.
No longer have I wanted to hold within my spleen.
The hate.
Since I was a kid I've tolerate.
There's no escape and I'm not running but
struggling to overcome of becoming.
The worse paradox that's on the spot.

Please you all I need to stop.
All I'm saying is I'm a ticking time bomb waiting to explode
at any moment and time when pushed to the limit.
Because like I said before my heart isn't in it.
But wait is something really wrong with me
that I need to do a "double take".
I guess like they say it's in your family traits.
But enough of this you all you have been dismissed.
By my angry but loving hug and kiss.
NOW SHOULD I GO AHEAD & EXPLODE!!!!

In this poem you'll get a lot of my anger and some of my immature ways and frustrations. It's funny how I look back at some of my poems they were very expressive and vivid. To think it wasn't all that long ago when I wrote it. So those of you that read this poem I hope you get the clarity and understanding of it. Also embrace the composition of this poem.

BLM
2011 THE SKIES THE LIMIT

My Prayer

Dear heavenly father.
Our Lord and savior.
That's pure within.
I need you in my life to cleanse my sins.
So I can become cleanse and pure within.

Don't want to keep washing up with impure thoughts.
But listen to God's pure thoughts that I've been once taught.
I have so many great leaders to thank like Moses, David, Solomon,
Martin Luther King Jr, Malcolm X, and Barack Obama.

But most importantly you heavenly father.
Because without you dear father.
We wouldn't have those great leaders to look up to as achievers.
We should and I should be your number #1 fan believer.
I never wanted to be in my own eyes your number #1 deceiver.

But like they say if one fails we all fail.
I just keep on keeping on to the wrong path.
I'm not studying hard enough to stay on the right path.
Just losing all the right skills in all the wrong places like math.
I'm just abusing the choices you gave me.
And those who have chosen to do wrong and not repent.

This prayer I'm saying is to show reverence.
And admit my mistakes.
Not to use every choice I can take as a second
but go with the right preference.
So I can take a second.
And let my progress be through you not me or man and say (Yes I Can).
No longer will I be controlled by man.
In Jesus name I pray amen.

BLM
2011 THE SKIES THE LIMIT

My Truth Is What
Side I'm Standing On

The truth is my heart is BIG on the inside.
Filled with the Holy Spirit.
On the outside.
But wait.
Which sides I'm standing on.
The left side or the right side.
Looking up at the sky at the bright side.

Praying to Jesus to direct me to the straight and
narrow which in my case is the right side.
Alright God.
I get you.
But not all of you.
To be true to myself.
And to get to know you.

You give us choices to either learn from or choose from.
Not to write flows to pick and choose from.
Especially to get recognition.
But that's our meaning my life's lesson.
It's so many questions.
But this is my confession wondering have I
learned anything as an adolescent.

To going in a Godly way.
Or to just do what I see fit.
It's okay.
That's not the way.
I think we all have been living that way.
Doing what we see fit to pass along the way.
But that's not okay.
Because I want Jesus passing along my way each and everyday.

I say everything for reason as I live by my words
simple and natural as breathing.
Please Jesus help us.
For we do not know what we do or better yet to do.

We are your children that's true but we are lost like loose screws.
Don't know where to look or turn.
And the simple answer would be you.
Most people are stubborn or really not trying to get to know you like me.
For example.
You gave me chance upon chances and still is.
But I'm not listening.
Instead I'm making goals and wishes.
Through me not through you.
So God the son, God the Holy Spirit, and God the father
help me because I do not know what I do or what to do.
Can you please tell me what side I'm standing
on before it's too late and I lose you?

BLM
2011 THE SKIES THE LIMIT

Life Is Like A Movie
C.S.S.

Lights, Camera's, & Action.
Have you ever thought about the deep meaning of life?
Well picture this as if we were in a movie.
Except we all play the major role.
And God is the director and narrator who's in control.

Here's the plot of the movie.
You normally have a good guy and a bad guy who's
generally trying to win the war or battle.
But this time it's a full view of everybody's secrecy.
Including comedy, romance, adventure, action,
horror, and just everyone's background.

So please shhh.
Don't make a sound the movie is playing in the full view audience.
That's in the background.
But it just amuses me everyone's character is just like reality tv.
Except you all playing yourselves.
As if you are on TV.
But it's Reality.
Like for instance there's Drama.
Everyone is a drama queen or king.
Well we all should get an Emmy award for that.

And everywhere you go there's drama that's not uncommon.
Then Action where there's a cause there's an
effect which causes an action.
Like making a movie the director has to say ACTION or CUT.

So far is everyone keeping up and good and ready in being
confused or saying huh, what now, come again.
Or you all just mumbling amongst yourselves up again.
Let me paint a picture that's a little quicker with words.
Everybody is always looking for a thrill or excitement
that gives you the chill and rush for adventure.
And keeps you proactive and in the picture.
How can I make it any more plain or simpler.

That's a brain buster like a fresh candy bag of GUSHERS.
If you all are ready to Ketchup and pay attention
as I spray my words that I Mustard.
Instead of you all not giving a person a chance
and just leave them alone and Flustered.
But it's a lot about this world that has to offer and take away.
Like being sadistic and twisted.
Only one word can give it away Horror.
Which people grasp the hunger for being scared and in
emotional pain in their demented sick minds.

This would drive the average person that's in their right mind insane.
Is everyone getting the concept and storing it in your cell membrane.
But just like (NIV) Romans 3:23 said.
For all have sinned and fall short of the glory of God.
This isn't no light switch where you can turn On and Off for God.
That would be odd.

But the things we do make it feel worthwhile.
Or okay to being sidetracked by the all knowing.
Like we laugh and cry.
And some people live and others die.
Just like you see in the movies knowing the unknowing.
And the motion pictures that's showing, the simplicity of it all.
Between scenes or behind or deleted scenes.
This isn't no longer an idea that you can dream.
It's the people who dream big dreams to making
it to reality or on the big screen.
Like when you see SEX on tv, or on the big screen.
Advertisements/billboards, and the public eye of the community.

This industry is messed up.
They mislead people to thinking or saying sex sells or
pornographic videos and images is the new romance.
When really it should be seen and called what it really is fornication.
There's no other translation for sex.

But don't forget this text.
Better yet save it as a monologue or a memory text.
This was not only a memory test.
It was a lesson for you to learn and study.
Just like entertainers study for their scenes.
To the movie manuscript.

Well that's what God wants is to do.
To study his word like a movie script.
This is just a trip.
For me because I'm not here to confront those who know what I know.
I'm also is here to confront my flaws and morals too.
That I no longer can continue to be a part of the interlude.
No people I'm not trying to be rude.
But I'm trying to inform and include.
You all God's people to live life to the fullest.
But in Jesus Christ our Lord.

So we all can be on one accord.
For our father, our lord, and savior.
This has been a Public Service Announcement is
anybody daring enough to stop me or yell Action.
Or should you all yell CUT.
YOU ALL DON'T GET IT I GUESS IM THE ONLY ONE.
THAT'S A WRAP FOLKS CUT.

I feel like this is one of the best poem I've ever written. I took the
time to think of it so I can create something so simple to become
so great. This poem describes every situation people go through in
the world and day to day life events. I believe that we all somehow
or another have a deep perception about life being full of drama
or like my poem in this case scenarios; "Life is like a Movie".

Who can say life is like a movie? That's why this poem means so much to me. To see how my progression has build intensity, suspense, and momentum; It has broaden my horizon and outlook on life. This poem will do all who read some justice and help you all. Happy reading!!!!

BLM
2011 THE SKIES THE LIMIT

Famous

I want to be famous.
The goals I'm looking forward to reaching isn't aimless.
But you all need to obtain this.
The meaning of what I mean to be famous.
Yeah there may be money, fame, and the public eye involved.

But it doesn't take rocket science.
Because I'm the math who's trying to get the fellow people involved.
And to solve the equations.
I want to help those in need.
Not take from the poor and give to the rich which we see on national tv.

What I really want is the national tv to see is me.
Helping those who can't help themselves.
That make more sense.
By doing so I'm making a difference in my
society better yet our universities.
It just hurts me.
What I can't do for the people I know or even see.
In my own community.

This is me speaking up or out for people to have faith in me.
As I strive for success and unity.
By taking on an act of kindness I'm also doing the work of Jesus to being
an absolution to the world's population to making a better solution.
Yeah what I'm doing is a struggle but didn't you all put
faith in the person that's in office with the muscle.

Well look at me like that.
"The man with a plan".
Which some people couldn't understand.
And put all the blame on one man.
But I'm in the stages of getting ready for the drama and the adversaries.
Even the people who label or pass judgment on me.
While the world faces adversity.

But this is me doing the opposite.
Being diverse or facing diversity.
I just need the people support and put their trust in me.
Like we do our money.
This is my step by step plan as a man of showing " yes we can" or "yes I can" be famous and make a difference.
After all reaching my goal of being famous isn't aimless.
Because I've been training for this.
Can I obtain this lifestyle because of the word famous.

Significance
C.S.S.

Who am I?
This black African American better known as a black guy.
Yes I.
Am a nice, well respectful, calm, cool, and collective guy.
But I'm not trying to boost up my echo.
It's more to the picture I'm painting.
I'm not claiming to be a hero.

Right now.
I'm feeling below ground zero.
But in society the only label they know is negro.
But the significance I'm bringing is to help our fellow people.
We should grow equally as a community (PEOPLE).

My spoken words are relevance.
To pertaining to significance to bringing out the magnificent.
But don't get these words I bent twisted.
Because the very point I make will slip over
your head and you will have miss it.

We need people to open up their senses.
And learn to pay close attention.
Like we do fresh buttermilk biscuits.
You see what I just did.
And they say tricks are for kids.
From start to finish.
I always finish what I start.
By winning over people's heart.
And finish what the average person couldn't start.
As the saying goes "don't try to put the cart before the horse".
Because my words are vivid like a (Charlie Horse).

You learn from your mistakes you have to of course.
Is this what it means to be significant or obtaining order of eloquence?
No this is just me being me the best I can be.
The greatest.
The magnificent.
So do you understand where I'm coming from and what I represent?
Because this is the best I could think of right now.
Censorship to my penmanship of the broad point of view I was making
my significance.

Have you ever wanted to write something so great that you didn't quite
know for sure that it would turn out so great? Well consider this; I
did it in this poem. Im so amazed and stunned at my own work and
when reading this poem it just takes me back to when I first wrote it.

This isn't your typical or average inspirational/creative poem. It
was a greater power within myself; I should say a super natural
power of GOD'S helping hand. He put the exact words and
combination together and made it flow. I'm truly and deeply
grateful for whatever reason I decided to write this poem.

I thank GOD mercifully and continuously for this gift of poetic
writing. This isn't the last of my true, and raw talent; there is
more, but this poem does and will always mean a lot to me.

I hope that when you read this; you also found
true amazement as I did when reading it.

Look At Me Now?

This was then.
And this is now.
Look at me now?
I was 18 then.
And now 23.
Look at me now?
I've made bad choices in life in the past but owning up to them now.
Look at me now?
Oh wow look at me some more I mean RIGHT NOW?

I dated someone 4 years younger than me to risking my life the agony
and pain to excluding everyone in my family just like when it rains.
Look at me now?
I was full rage willing and ready to be released
and unlocked from my emotional cage.
Look at me now?

Here I am 19.
Treated as if I was 15.
Look at me now?
The year 2008 I've graduate.
Look at me now?
Still not satisfied I'm feeling petrified with myself and nothing else
matter to me or understanding the things that comes to me now.
Look at me now?

I'm 20 now no backing down enrolled to job corp as
if I'm reenlisting myself to the marine corp.
Look at me now?
I was never fighter then but more a fighter now.
Look at me now?

Hit the LOTTO oops nope just 21 my age but my writing experiences
will make up the differences to my anger as to my rage.
To coming and leaving from being in relationships.
Or just being single.
To realizing what's the real meaning of mingle is.
But I'm not the person to bite on my words but just the chips PRINGLES.
Giving you all my whole life story bits and pieces
like it was my very first hit single.
Look at me now?

Just turned 22 still have a lot of loose screws
and trying to figure out what to do.
Aiming to be Christ like but seeing so much of the lime light
instead of falling on my knees praying to Jesus to deliver me.
Look at me now?
I've been given a second chance not once but 7x70
so I can sit down and listen to my calling.
Because I'm falling.
And everyone else is around me is also.
Not to judge or discourage anybody.
I'm not the person to say.
I told you so or I thought so.
Look at me now?

23 now and living for the now like my life depending on it RIGHT NOW.
Look at me now?
No more looking over my shoulder or turning my
head but staying on the straight and narrow.
Now and imagine what lies beyond and what's ahead.
Look at us now?
Heaven the new order of things as to the christening age.
Look at him now?

I been kicked when I was down.
Bullied round and round.
Wasn't a class clown.
Just a clown in class.
Look at me now?

I ask Jesus questions.
He ask God for the solutions.
My mind and body I was polluting.
With earth garbage.
Myself worth is more than an arm pit.
I was made to believe I was different.
Look at me now?
I have no direction.
But I'm looking for perfection.
My insecurities made me question myself.
Asking God for help.
All the wealth in the world is meaningless.
Without Jesus and peace of mind.
Now I'm bout to give u a piece of my mind.
Look at me now?

No matter how fast I can run, I can never run away.
From my problems.
My life was 1 big problem.
Grew up a fatherless child.
Afraid to invest in myself.
Crying out for help.
But no one hears me.
Look at me now.

A 24 year old male.
A wolf in sheep clothing.
Was molded into an image that is false.
Trying to break out this prison, Enter the gates of heaven.
Look at me now?

I made so many mistakes.
Its bigger than a mountain.
I'm not counting.
Held hostage by depression.
But who cares.
I'm not going to throw an officer out of his patrol car.
So I'm not going to cop out.
Look at me now?

I know I can make a difference.
I know there's no problem too big.
That God can't handle.
Look at me now?

BCM & BLM
2012 I WILL PREVAIL

Back In Business

Back in affect.
Whether there's a cause there's an effect.
Because I'm taking action for my life.
You live on.
You live strong.
Because "I'm on One" like Drake.
Not to influence those as suppose to a mixtape.
Because I'm a ape.
Meaning I'm in beast mode.
This isn't Morse code.

I'm tired of being sick and tired of speaking in dialogue as to a
monologue to reaching my point across my foolish ways and emotions.
Sticking two fingers up my index and my middle.
Chalking up duces.
Everyday, of every second, to every minute, to the hour
my strength loosens and I'm feeling stupid.

No this isn't me trying to be Cupid.
This is the REAL so let me introduce those
who don't know the REAL me.
The DEAL because I'm so ILL mentally.
So Lord feel me.
With your everlasting love, & spirit.
I'm asking point blank period.
Humble me.
Feel me with the Holy Ghost.
Because I no longer want to feel like an empty seed to a ghost.
Even get trapped into the material things of power, money,and greed.

But raising my glass up.
To presenting a toast.
Because like i said before I'm on ONE.
To feeling God in my life as to the Holy Ghost.
I'm telling you all this because I'm back in business.
So get with my BUSINESS.
Do you all get this?

BLM
2012 I WILL PREVAIL

Humble Me Lord

Lord I know I tend to say, think, and react to the
wrong actions, disagreements, and situations.
But you know my heart.
Which you know is a working progress.
For me to live and breathe.
The "Humble me Lord" process.

Everyday is a test.
And your not my number one guess.
Which comes to mind.
But as I live and breathe.
Put in my veins that I bleed.
The humble me lord rhymes that you put in mind.
Lord its about that time to be fully committed and submit to you.
Not once a day, or a minute, or moment, or two but every day.

I want to have patiences.
Be zealous.
Show meekness.
And utilize my uniqueness.
But before I go on.
I want to develop a stronger relationship with you first.
To seek this.
Because God you know this sinful world is my sickness to falling
down to not having a strong will which is my weakness.
So Lord listen while I speak this.

I'm a sinner no doubt about it.
So Lord the only question is?
What am I going to do about it?
Lord help me I want to fall in love with you first.

Because I don't want to end up like Lucifer.
Who condemned and cursed this earth.
And leaving it worse for better.
Instead of better not for worse events at all.

Your the number one guy, person, and God I
want to call my everything my all.
Humble me Lord.
I want to die to myself and in return it will be my life's gain.
To burn the sins i haven't shaken but awaken.
To relieve myself with God's help.
This sinful pain.

Lord humble me through all eternity, through the
rough times, floods, storms, and good times.
Let him reign as I take your love of my soul to my heart.
Also to my brain.
Humble me Lord.
Willingly and truthfully forever in your name
my prayer in Jesus name AMEN.

BLM
2012 I WILLING PREVAIL

Poetic Justice

Does it do me any justice for all y'all who look up to me.
That read some of my old than again new poetry.
Let's call it what my title is "Poetic Justice".
Hate it or love it.
Taking my creative action to the public just
giving it all back to the republic.

Because I'm serving everybody with poetic justice.
People can't touch this.
I see people frowning and drowning then see
people go from smiling to hollin.
When really I'm trying to keep the balance.
With all the negativity that we all see.

Then challenge people that read my sometimes depressing,
critical, etc but mainly uplifting poetry.
So all of us that cope with society and the head/
tails of problems that come with it.
So it can keep us well rounded and grounded.

This is a new light for me living life like it's golden.
Because each and every year I'm going to be growing.
No more reaping what I'm sowing.
Or creeping over peoples toes and.
But living life as it comes and as it goes.
Going with flow.
You already know what comes next poetic and my justice.

Because what's going on in the world.
It really needs a lot of justice.
As to my poetic justice best believe and trust this.

BLM
2012 I WILL PREVAIL

4 More Years

Guess what you all?
The pain is gone.
We have 4 more years so quit your crying and tears.
Barack Obama made it through his first term of
presidency now going in his second term.
Don't catch fire in your hair with the burn of the perm.

Because now it's the democratic's turn.
But mainly blacks to put our names on and
off the map to make a difference.
So sit back and take a listen because this isn't
what the Republicans been wishing for.
I'm not done yet just getting started forgetting
where we all came from to wanting more.
I see why now as a black man what Barack Obama's slogan was saying.
"YES WE CAN".
Go forward to make a change.

To following TuPac in his music that "it wasn't
heaven sent to not seeing a black president.
To following Dr. Martin Luther King which I think
God played a roll of him predicting the future.
To seeing where we all stand now for the future.
I pay homage and tribute to President Barack
Obama for being the first black president.

To fixing what seems to be a endless curse of
United States of America (USA).
With the whole world sitting in God's hands.
To seeing 4 more years of change for all humanity.
And it stand.
As a supporter of the Change foundation.
And President Obama I approve this message.
So sit back and relax embrace it.
And just take it in.
Because this is 2013 to making it 4 more years of change.
It's that simple and plain.

BLM
2013 Pursuing The Dream

So Proud

Say it out loud.
I'm so proud.
I finally made it.
I finally did it.
Do this mean I'm on the stepping stone to be being committed.
Feeling so accomplished and bless.
Not rockin the sign (S).
Meaning stress on my chest.

Better yet living life as it is a big test.
And rockin Polo.
Oh no but yes.
And just take a guess?
What's in my wallet?
You right the name brand GUESS that's in my pocket.
Just flowing off my tibia as my words in nuclear to drop as an atom bomb.
To positive thinking.

To just thinking where have my mind been.
Since the last 5 years of thinking.
I must have been drinking.
To being overdose to seeing so many people comatose.
But this isn't a ROAST.
Its me being proud to being black and me saying it out loud.

This goes out to the crowd.
Of people that's been supporting me since I wasn't
at the legal age of drinking or smoking.
To now sit back and relax to see my work come to progress.
And look at my true success.
And this isn't gone be laid to rest.
I'm so proud.
So wont you be the judge.
Or my fans to saying it for me.
OUT LOUD I'M SO PROUD.

BLM
2013 Pursuing the Dream

Wanting More

Go Hard.
Or go Home.
Because ever since i started writing poetry.
I wanted to exceed to my fullest potential.
From watching "Home Alone".
To leaving from school to coming home alone.

It was said best by Mr. T.
"I pity a Fool".
And the thugs out on the street slanting the drugs
on the corners thinking they cool.
Please don't make me act rude.
Because they don't know what's the very next
word that comes out my mouth.
Could be the results of attitude.
Leaving you all shocked with your mouths open and full of dribble drool.
Want more or me.
Leaving you all wanting more.
This isn't a detour but a tour of envisions.
To my intuition.
Not having cruel intentions.
But me working hard to the hourly grind.
Are you all ready to see me shine?
Wanting more stay inturned for more.
To be continued....

BLM
2013 Pursuing the Dream

Special Thanks
& Tributes

Mrs. Lynn M. Connelly- For pushing me to pursue my ambitions, with my writing poetry, and as well as helping me with I find most important my speech and vocabulary. I thank you. You are a true inspiration to me as a teacher, & philosopher. You molded me into something amazing and that wont go unnotice you are a true cargiver. You are my favorite teacher and I dedicate this book to you most of all.

Sean D. Morgan Bell- I thank you for being a friend, older brother, father figure, and mentor for the many of years to me. As well as listening to the many poems I have written. And just being there for me when I needed you or someone to talk to for advice or just understing life period. I thank you love you man. You help raise me to be the man I became today.

Bartholomew C. Moorman-We've always been close and I would just about do anything for you. I'm glad you were apart of the good/bad journeys with me. Thanks for contributing to my book as well as your ideas, talents, and inputs. You deserve every bit of this book project. I hope you will keep up your gifts/ talents and be apart of more future projects with me.

Portrait Innovations

Glenville S.D.A.Church/The Outside

MyRon Edmonds

Any and everyone who I missed or failed to mention family friends thank you all for your support.

Printed in the United States
By Bookmasters